If Jonah Had a Wife

Revised Edition

theunknownprophet22@gmail.com

*To Jonah, the one true and perfect prophet
who was swallowed by a fish.*

Contents

Author's Note

If Jonah Had a Wife parallels to my life—all of the things that happened to Jonah in my book happened to me in real life except I did not get swallowed by a big fish. On the other hand, I had worse things happen to me. This book is so important because it is about the kingdom of God that Jesus preached. Jesus said when the kingdom of God is preached all over the world then he is coming back; this book is about the book of revelation. That is what is amazing about my book. The Lord told me about this book and the prophecy that is happening right now. When you read *If Jonah Had a Wife,* you will see this book is about Jesus coming back to Earth again because there was only one man Jesus compared himself to and that was the prophet, Jonah. Jonah is the good guy I am the only preacher that shows that Jonah is the good guy and not the bad guy.

You can easily reach out to the author for speaking engagement inquiries by contacting via email at theunknownprophet22@gmail.com

Chapter 1

Jonah's Picnic

It was a beautiful summer afternoon with the most spectacular event that everyone looked forward to – the biggest picnic by the seaside, beautiful trees, A sandy beach, a slight breeze in the air with trees and shades! Everyone came to this event, especially the congregational leaders of all the surrounding towns 400 miles away. Jonah's wife and two children, Luke, their 15-year-old son and Kimberly, their 12-year-old daughter, were setting at the picnic table under the shade of a tree.

This was the biggest feast anyone had ever seen. The table had big bowls of fried chicken, mashed potatoes and gravy, stuffed eggs, chicken and dumplings, corn on the cob, and baked beans. The tables were filled with homemade fruit pies and homemade cakes.

Rebecca was feeling nervous and out of place because she did not know where Jonah had gone. Then, two ladies from the congregational society came over to Rebecca's table and said, "We need to talk to you about Jonah. If there's any way we can help you, we will. We know the anguish and the pain that Jonah is causing you. We don't believe he's a true prophet of God; he does not support you and take care of your children. He does not get food for you, he does not pay your bills. We are sad for you; the little shack that you live in has holes in the wall, your roof leaks, you don't have very good heat to keep you warm and you hardly have enough food to eat. Where is Jonah?"

Rebecca, lifting up her head looked at the two ladies and said, "I think he ran off and found another woman. I know that he hates me!"

They replied, "We need you to talk to the leader of the congregation. We are willing to give you some more food and help you some but this cannot continue. You have to have someone that's able to take care of you and work for you and Jonah is not doing what God wanted him to do and is not taking care of his family. God would not call a man to be a prophet and then neglect his own family and not feed them and give them a good house to live in. Here comes Balak, the leader of the congregation."

"Hi. We hope you are enjoying the picnic in the bountiful supply of food. We have let Jonah in the congregation in the past but if he comes back, we will have him exiled from our presence. He is no longer allowed to speak in our presence. Yes, some of the things he prophesied, it would appear that some of those came to pass but we believe it was a coincidence! Some people claim that they received miracles. One lady said she was blind; Jonah prayed for her and she could see. We think she made up the whole story and she's lying. We want you to tell Jonah that if he does come back and come to our congregational meeting, we will have the soldier security put him in jail. Jonah is not called by God, he is a false prophet! Certain regions in Jerusalem still regard him as a true prophet of God but we do not. His last prophecy said that God told him to go to Nineveh; God would not tell Jonah to go to Nineveh; they are the enemies of God! We believe Jonah is a traitor and went to Nineveh to be on their side. How do you feel about this Rebecca?"

"I think my husband hates me anyway. I will tell you what happened two weeks ago. After Jonah prophesied to the congregation and told everyone that God told him to go to Nineveh and tell them they were going to be destroyed in 40 days, he asked me to cook some bacon and eggs. He was getting ready to go. I told him God would not tell him to go to Nineveh and tell them they were going to be destroyed and leave his family. But he packed his luggage, loaded things up in the wagon, teamed up the horses and said that we could go with him to Joppa Bay, where he was going to get on a ship. I kept asking Jonah when he would be back. He said he did not know, and went inside the ticket office and bought a ticket. Kimberly and Luke were crying they did not want their dad to leave them alone. I said 'You're just leaving me to go find another woman.'" He turned back and looked at me and said, "No I am not leaving to find another woman. If I wanted another woman, I would find one here. There are a lot of women here. I have told you God spoke to me and told me to go to Nineveh and say these exact words that they will be destroyed in 40 days. Then I saw Jonah quickly get onto the ship but it started sailing toward Tarsus. Then I screamed, 'You lied to me you're not going to Nineveh!'"

Ballak put his right hand on Rebecca's shoulder and said, "God has always destroyed his enemies, Noah's flood, Pharaoh's army, Sodom and Gomorrah. As you know, God would not send a prophet to Nineveh; God is going to destroy those people. So Jonah has prophesied and said when he gets there to Nineveh that they are going to be destroyed in 40 days. You'll see he is a false prophet when Nineveh is not destroyed. We want you to know we don't blame you Rebecca. Enjoy the picnic; we will see you at the congregation service on Sunday.”

Luke and Kimberly quickly said, “Mom, can we go down to the seashore and play in the water?”

“Yes it's okay, just don't get too close to the water. You can make sand castles but don't get in the water.”

Looking over at Kimberly, she was building a sand castle near the seashore when all of a sudden a big fish came up out of the water with a loud noise, and a big man came out of the fish's mouth

“Look it's a monster!” the women started screaming. The man picked up spears and the soldiers grabbed their spears and started running toward this monster on the beach. It's a big fish monster and the monster came out of his mouth. Kill them both!! The soldiers ran quickly and surrounded this sea monster. The leader of the soldiers raised up his spear and pointed toward the fish and said, “On my command, kill it.” Then suddenly Jonah, being very weak and sick, lifted up one hand and said, "Wait it's me Jonah the prophet. Don't kill me." Jonah's son Luke was nearby and said, "That's Dad, don't hurt him, and Luke started crying, "That's Jonah my dad." Luke ran over and took a hold of Jonah's hand and said, "Dad are you okay?"

The leader of the soldier said, "Standdown it is a man." Luke looked up to the soldiers, crying, "Please help my dad." They picked up Jonah and started carrying him up to the picnic tables. The leader of the soldier said, "Kill that fish. We'll cook that for supper tomorrow." But the fish turned and splashed back into the ocean and swam away.

Chapter 2

Jonah Accused

Jonah, the prophet, was very weak and could not stand up by himself. Balak, the congregational leader, commanded the soldiers to take Jonah before the Council. They took Jonah to a room and gave him some food from the picnic so that he could get strong enough to answer the allegations.

Jonah ate some food and went to sleep. He was too weak to be questioned. He lay there resting for two days and then was strong enough to talk to the Council. Balak stood up and questioned Jonah and said to him, "You know that you have sinned against God. That's why this trouble has come on you. If you would repent and make things right, we would allow you to be in our congregation once again. You have sinned against God because you don't take care of your family, you have lied to us, and you are not a true prophet of God. We need you to repent and tell the truth. You lied to your wife, you told her you were going to Nineveh but you got on a ship to go to Tarshish. Why would God tell you to go to Nineveh and tell them that they will be destroyed in 40 days? Tell us why."

Then Jonah stood up and put his hand on the rail so he would not fall over. "I will tell you why God chose me to be his prophet and called me. God spoke to me and told me to go to Nineveh because God loves everyone. God loves me and I love God. God even wants us to love our enemies. The Council quickly stood up. You can't say that in this house. That is against God's word, and you lied and said you were going to Nineveh and you went the other way."

Jonah lifted up his eyes and quickly looked at the Council and said, "You don't kill people, you don't torture people, you don't beat people but you have no love for people. You don't prove that you love God. You show no love to anyone, you don't know God because God is love, God only calls love. There's no love in this Council or this congregation."

The Council stood up and quickly said, "You love Nineveh, our enemies that kill our relation." Jonah quickly spoke, "I will tell you this one thing so you understand why I did not go immediately to Nineveh! This is how much love God has for all the people he created. I knew when I got to Nineveh and cried against them and I prophesied they would be destroyed in 40 days, I knew you would call me a false prophet because they would not be destroyed. God would spare their life and save them. I knew that if I did not go to Nineveh, God would save the Ninevites. I will go to my house and I will rest and when God speaks to me again and tells me to go to Nineveh, I will get up and I will quickly go to Nineveh and give the prophecy to the Ninevites. I have prophesied God's word many times. All prophecies I prophesied came to pass. They all came true. If you could send your love to the enemy nation and it would save them and stop them from being evil and help them, would you have? No, you want to see people die. I will tell you what happened to me. God prepared the fish, and the fish swallowed me. I was in the fish's belly for three days and three nights. I thought that I was going to die. I cried out to God because I know God loves me and he made the fish puke at your picnic.

The Council stood up and said, "You have insulted the house of the congregation, the doctrines of our bylaws and the constitutional rights in whereby we believe in God. It is the decision of this Council you are not allowed to come back. If you come back in our congregation, we will have you arrested and put in jail." Jonah started slowly walking toward the door and said, "I love all of you none of you love me."

Jonah walked out of the building and went home. Rebecca was cooking some baked beans on the stove. Jonah laid down. Rebecca came into the room and said, "See, Jonah you've made me look like a fool.

The congregation says that you're worse than an infidel because you won't feed your family! All the other ladies have a leopard skin fur coat but not me because you never have time to go kill a leopard cat. That's not asking too much for you to go and do."

Jonah looked at her and said, "Rebecca if it means that much to you, when I wake up, I'll go on a leopard cat hunt. I'll get you a leopard skin. God will speak to me again and tell me to go to Nineveh. This time I will go to Nineveh, that great city and cry against them."

Rebecca said to Jonah, "Will you really get me the leopard skin coat?"

"I will get it for you Rebecca."

She continued cooking baked beans for supper. Early the next morning, Jonah was feeling good. He got up and got his things together to go find a leopard cat to kill. Rebecca looked at him and said sarcastically, "The fur coat, if you can get one, is not going to make up for everything else because I know you really hate me and God hates me. Everyone hates me!!!!"

Jonah was gone for five hours. When he came back, he was dragging the biggest leopard cat you had ever seen. He hung it up in the tree and cut it up and cut the fur off of the leopard cat and took it down to the first tanner that fixed up the leopard coat. Jonah's arms were all cut up from the leopard cat. When Rebecca was in somewhat of a shock, she said, "What happened to you Jonah?" He looked at her and said, the cat cut me all up. I don't know how to fight a cat."

With Jonah's arms bleeding, Rebecca quickly ran and got rags and wrapped them around Jonah's arms to stop the blood. Jonah healed up pretty well in two days. God spoke to Jonah the next morning. Jonah arose and went to Nineveh the second time and cried against those wicked people. Jonah said, "Yes Lord, I will go." He got his horse and started heading toward Nineveh on land.

Chapter 3

Shipmates

Jonah was traveling for two days on his way to Nineveh. In the cool of the evening, he came to a little brook and built a campfire for the evening. Jonah was cooking his supper when he heard two men approaching. The two men said to Jonah, "Can we share your campfire for the night?" Jonah smiled happily and said, "Yes, please I would enjoy the company; you're welcome!!"

The man said, "My name is Jenkins; this is my brother William." They sat down and had some coffee and began to eat supper. Jenkins said, "If you don't mind me asking, what happened to your skin. It looks like you've been severely burnt." William quickly said, "You know your voice sounds familiar. I think we have met somewhere before. Could you tell us your name?

Jonah looked at the two men and said, "Yes my name is Jonah."

William stood up very quickly and said, "I can't believe it. We wondered what happened to you. I was the shipmaster on the ship that you got on at Joppa Bay. And this is William, he was my first mate. We wondered if you died that day when we threw you out of the ship. We heard rumors but I can't believe it. We're sitting here talking to you. You're alive!!!!"

William said to Jonah, "That was a terrible storm. We owe our lives to you Jonah. You saved our lives that day, because we now serve your God, the God that created the heavens and the earth and the sea and the mountains."

Jonah looked at Jenkins and said, "That is wonderful. I'm glad I am on my way to Nineveh to cry against that wicked city. God told me to go to Nineveh and tell them in 40 days, they are going to be overthrown. The prophets committee from Jerusalem, and the king of Jerusalem all want Nineveh people to be destroyed. I stood before the Council at Jerusalem and told them God was going to spare their life, God loves all people and God would have mercy on the Ninevites. Yes, God told me to say these exact words that they will be overthrown in 40 days, that God is a loving God and he loves all people. They call me a false prophet; they say I'm contradicting myself. If I say they will be overthrown in 40 days and the Ninevites are not destroyed, then I am a false prophet!!!!"

William looked at Jonah and said, "People are saying that you were running away from God and did not want to be God's prophet anymore and you were trying to run away from his presence, we know that you love God. Jonah, we know that your God's prophet, God came after you only because he wants you with him."

Jonah glanced down at the fire. And looked at the flames for A moment, and looked back at the shipmates with the light from the fire in his eyes. "You know the truth, I was not going to Tarsus to get away from God because I know that the presence of God is with me all the time. I know I'm secure and saved by God's grace and mercy. I know that God loves me. The Council at Jerusalem wants to kill me. I am not afraid to die; I am not afraid to be killed for serving God. The Jerusalem Council said I did not even hear God's voice. I want Nineveh people to be spared and to be saved. I am not afraid of the Ninevites. I know they will not hurt me. I know that if I don't go to the Nineveh, God will spare their life, God will save them."

William spoke up loudly, "We know you're not afraid because you told us to throw you in the raging sea.

Jenkins said, "We know how much you love us because you did not want us to get hurt in the storm. We would be honored if you let us walk with you all the way to Nineveh. We are going there to buy supplies to take back to our ship."

Then Jonah said, "Yes we are two weeks away from Nineveh. I would like to explain to you why I went to Joppa Bay and got on a ship instead of going to Nineveh the first time!"

Jenkins spoke up very quickly, "You don't owe us any explanation. We know that you are a true right prophet of God, but we would love to hear what happened if you would like to tell us.then Jonah said I knew that the Ninevites were going to be kind to me. When I got there, I knew that they were going to repent and serve God. It's my own people at Jerusalem; they're the ones that show hate. They are the ones saying they want me dead and I am a false prophet I was not running from God; I was running from Jerusalem. I did not want to go back to the people that claim to be my people and accuse me falsely that I am a false prophet."

Jenkins said can ask you one more question before we go to sleep. People said, "You prayed a prayer when you were in the fish's belly and you said they that observe lying vanities forsake their own mercies; can you tell us what you meant by praying that? Yes, people in the synagogue and the High Council in Jerusalem put white robes on and make long prayers. They say they are right with God but they are not. They say they hear from God but God does not talk to them; that is a lying vanity. They get dressed up in fancy clothes; they have gold jewelry, fancy things. They think because they have all of this, they are in God's will. They prophesy things, but God did not tell them to prophesy They want to look important and better than everyone, this is a lying vanity. I knew then it's better to be in a fish's belly and know that you are a true prophet of God and that God spoke to you than to have all of those riches and not hear from God, and God's love with you. Good night."

Chapter 4

Jonah arrives at Nineveh

Jonah arrived at Nineveh and immediately began to preach, in 40 days, you will be overthrown. Jonah walked into the city of Nineveh preaching with a loud voice, yet in 40 days, you will be overthrown.

Yet 40 days and Nineveh shall be overthrown. Jonah had walked into Nineveh on a full day's journey when there were a lot more people together. They said who is this man? Why is he telling us this? Jonah made sure that he preached exactly the words that God told him to say. Jonah did not tell Nineveh to repent, or in 40 days, they would be overthrown. Jonah told them exactly what God told him to say, yet

40 days and Nineveh shall be overthrown. Jonah saw the magnificent buildings, the gold, the riches, the environment of the town, the spectacular buildings and modernization of living in houses, the smell of food cooking in the air!

A storekeeper came running out of his business and quickly said, "This is a prophet of God who created the world. This is the man who was swallowed by a fish and lived! Quickly go tell the king."

Jonah was offered some food, and he accepted. He ate and rested momentarily, quickly got up and continued. Yet in 40 days, Nineveh shall be overthrown. Some people approached Jonah and said, "What right do you have to tell us that Nineveh will be overthrown?" Jonah ignored them and kept yelling louder preaching, in 40 days Nineveh shall be overthrown. Then as Jonah reached the far-east side of Nineveh, loud cries was throughout the city. The king declared a fast. The king of Nineveh said, "Let's all fast, no food, no water and repent and ask God to spare us."

Jonah walked to the mountain that overlooked Nineveh. He built him a little hut and set in the shadows. God prepared a gourd plant that grew up and extended farther out of his house and gave him more shade when the sun came up it was very hot. Jonah was looking toward Nineveh to see what the people would do. When God grew the plant the gourd, they gave him more shade. He was very happy; he felt like maybe he could even make this his home, instead of going back to Jerusalem; no one wanted to see him, and no one wanted him to come back; he was all alone! Then God made a worm that went into the gourd and it ate the gourd. Jonah had no more shade. Jonah, the prophet, prayed; he then stood up and he knew it was okay with God if he went back to Nineveh. On his way through, he could find work; people would help him and give him food there. God revealed to Jonah that day how much he wanted to supply all of his needs with the house, food and everything that Jonah needed to live. Jonah quickly entered Nineveh. Some of the Ninevites had already started forming a congregation to make sacrifices and an altar to the God of heaven, the God that created the heavens and the earth. They welcomed Jonah again and gave him a place to live. They gave him food and took him before the king. He was very grateful and thanked him that their city was spared the king of Nineveh ask Jonah what he would like to do, Jonah stayed as the prophet over the congregation. The congregation grew, and people experienced for the first time what it was like to love each other and to worship the one true God. Not all people of Nineveh love God. There was a conspiracy; some wanted to kill Jonah they wanted to remove him. They falsely accused him of being a spy from Jerusalem to take over and secretly tear down the Ninevites' Empire.

A beautiful lady came up to Jonah, brought him a cake, and told Jonah that she was in love with him and wanted to be his wife. Jonah looked at her auburn hair and was amazed. He was lonely and loved the way she talked and the way she looked. They set by the fireplace looking at the stars and the moon, talking of wonderful and sweet things Jonah said, "I'm sorry I cannot marry you. I want you to be my wife. I am still married to Rebecca, and I must go back to see if I can work things out with her to see if she will love me and like me!"

The most beautiful lady I have ever seen put her gentle hand on mine and, looked into my eyes and begged me, "You know that it would be perfect if I were your wife. I would make you happy. I will cook for you. I would do everything for you." Jonah looked deep into her eyes and said, you are truly the lady that I've always looked for. I like your name more then any then I've ever heard because her name was Honey.

Honey quickly responded to Jonah and said, "I know you're a true prophet of God I will go anywhere with you." Honey looked to Jonah again and said, "Please send a messenger to your wife Rebecca and tell her you want me to be your wife. The anguish that you've gone though, she does not believe that you're true prophet of God and by our laws Jonah you can have more than one wife."

Jonah responded back to Honey and said, "That's just it. I don't want more than one wife. I want to make sure that I'm doing the right thing." They curled up by the fireplace and fell fast asleep with Honey embracing in Jonah's arms, the smell of the meat coming on the campfire. When Jonah and Honey woke up the next morning, he was preparing for his journey. He turned to Honey and said, "I will do it. I will send back a messenger and I will tell Rebecca that we will no longer be husband-and-wife. Moses allowed divorces because she does not believe in God and she does not serve the God that created the heaven and the earth."

Honey started jumping up and down with joy and gladness, telling Jonah how much she loved him, when all of a sudden, some soldiers came from Nineveh and grabbed a hold of Honey. They were dragging her away; they said Jonah had committed high treason against Jerusalem. "We do not acknowledge his authority as a prophet of God. Take Jonah to jail." They took Honey to her mom and dad's house and put her in temporary holding so that she could not go out of the house until she forgot about Jonah the prophet.

Jonah was heartbroken, and they put him in jail for two days. He was crying out because his heart was broken because of how much he fell in love with Honey. They released Jonah and told him that he was exiled from Nineveh. The Council had more authority even though the king ruled and said that they would serve God, the king himself did not have enough authority to grant Jonah to live in Nineveh full-time. The king secretly met Jonah and gave him a bag of gold and said you are always welcome with me.

Then the king said one last thing to Jonah, "I believe your God that you serve will show you the way of deliverance and you will get everything you need. Jonah thanked the king very much they embraced and hugged each other. Jonah told the king he loved him and his family and headed back to Jerusalem. Jonah knew that he was never going to be able to marry Honey because of the Council in Nineveh. As he thought about it and went on his journey, maybe this last time I could be in love with Rebecca and she would be happy with me. Jonah went to the telegraph office, where they have a very fast, speedy mail delivery service. He sent a message with a rider ahead to go to Rebecca as fast as they could and let her know that he was on his way back to see his son Luke and his daughter Kimberly.

Chapter 5

Jonah's trip back to Jerusalem

Jonah travelled for two days toward Jerusalem. At 5 o'clock in the evening. He came to a camp of 25 people having a prayer meeting. When Jonah got near the people, the leader named Luther said, "Please, stranger, come in and join us!" Jonah could smell all the wonderful food cooking on their campfire. Luther said, "You're welcome to the Bible study and when we get done, have a feast with us. Jonah quickly said, "Thank you very much. That food smells great!!!!", they did not recognize Jonah the prophet. Luther said, "Would you join hands with us? We would like to pray and we would like to pray for you too if that's okay? But before we pray, we want you to know we are missionaries on our way to Nineveh to start a ministry there since Jonah the prophet went there and preached the city, repented and turned to God!!!!" Then Luther began to pray. God spoke to Luther. Luther walked over towards Jonah and not knowing who he was, he put his hand on his head. God is giving me a word to tell you. He said you are going to be great; you are great in the eyes of God; you are going to be rich and famous, preaching all over the world and singing!"

Jonah lifted up his hands, tears running down his cheek and they were all jumping up and down and dancing with joy. Jonah, with a loud voice, said yes, that is true. They set back down by the fire. They asked Jonah, "Would you tell us your name?" He said, "Yes I will. I am Jonah, the prophet that went to Nineveh." They were all excited about the presence of revival. They were shouting and jumping up and down, hugging Jonah, saying, "We wondered what happened to you. We know you are a true man of

God. Please tell us what happened. We know you were swallowed by a fish. Please tell us what happened on the boat and what happened in Nineveh after the king declared to repent, and God said he repented and did not overthrow Nineveh."

"Yes I will tell you what happened to me. I did not run from God; I did not run from the presence of God. They said that about me; I did not say that. I will tell you the true reason why I went to Joppa Bay and got on a ship to go to afar city to Tarshish. I was running from Jerusalem and the false prophets and the false king. They're rich, they have much gold, many cattle, they have everything but they do not serve God. They do not worship God. They say that about me because I have no money or nothing, I am not a true prophet of God, then when I was in Nineveh and I preached for three days across the big city and I went up on the hill, I heard the city repent and cry out to God that he would not overthrow their city. And God gave me a gift and gave a shade that grew up and God told me that the Ninevites had many cattle and that I was his prophet and I would leave there and God was going to give me cattle and gold and many wonderful things I have never had anything but God told me then I was his prophet I knew God loves me and I love God, and now you did not know who I was! And you spoke the word of prophecy to me that God told me on the mountain."

Luther said, "Please tell us what happened when you got swallowed by a big fish. Did you think you were going to die?" Jonah stood up and looked at the people and said, "When I got on the ship at Joppa Bay, I immediately went down below and went to sleep it was so peaceful that I was resting really nice when the wave started rocking the boat I was asleep very sound when the storm came and shaking the boat when the ship captain woke me up and told me to come up to the top of the ship or they was all going to be destroyed, I knew why the storm came and I told all the shipmates I said I am Jonah the prophet I serve the most high God that created the heaven and the earth I told all the men to throw me out of the ship but the reason why I told these men to throw me out of the ship was because I am a good swimmer and I knew I could swim to the shore I would not have drowned but if I would have just jumped out of the ship by myself with the waves beating against the ship then I would have been killed because the wave would've slammed my body against the ship I was not asking them to kill me. When the shipmates understood this, they were glad to help me. They just wanted to make sure that I would be okay and not get hurt. People said that I wanted to commit suicide. Some said that I would rather die instead of going to Nineveh to preach, but it was not that at all, I wanted the Ninevites to be saved, I wanted everyone to be saved; I knew already if I did not go to Nineveh, God was going to spare the city of the Ninevites but God chose me to go to preach and I did that. Every time that I prophesied in the past, Jerusalem got rich, they got lots of money, they got lots of gold, they got lots of cattle. Every time I prophesied, somebody else gets wealth and riches and everything! But they observe lying vanities and they forsake their own mercies and now when I preach to Nineveh in 40 days, they will be overthrown. They all knew what I prophesied and they were going to call me a false prophet because that did not come to pass; God spoke to me in Nineveh and showed me that I would have many cattle and the time has come to go back to Jerusalem, that I will see this prophecy for my own life, and then thank you Luther that you obey God spoke to me confirming prophecy that God had already spoke to me."

Chapter 6

Jonah's Disguise

The next morning, Luther and Jonah and the missionaries said goodbye they continued on to Nineveh. Then when they were gone, God spoke to Jonah again and said, "Jonah arise and cut off your beard and fashion your hair in this certain way. You will look like a new man when you get into Jerusalem. This will be a new look for you because I have called you into a new ministry and a new way. When you arrive in Jerusalem, go and buy your new clothes that no one would think you would wear, and a new horse and buggy. Then go and see your wife Rebecca buy new furniture and fix her house, and then tell her you will get a divorce. Then get a new job with the cargo company hauling supplies and goods to different cities from Jerusalem to leave your buggy with Rebecca until you return. You will be in the transportation business for now."

Jonah knew if he told any of the congregation these words, he would be ridiculed. Jonah continued traveling toward Jerusalem with anticipation, knowing that if he entered the city, no one would recognize him; his skin had healed up, and he looked like a different man. No one would walk up to him and say, "Hey, you're Jonah, the prophet and start saying bad things to him."

Jonah quickly got back to Jerusalem and went and bought a new buggy that God told him to do. He bought new clothes, and dressed up; he felt like he was on cloud nine. Jonah went to the supermarket to buy some groceries to take back to Rebecca. He thought maybe he would give it one more chance with Rebecca to see if it would work out if it did they would both be happy. When Jonah was in the supermarket, he bought some flowers for Rebecca. Walking down an aisle, he saw a pretty lady standing there. He thought, *I think I will talk to her just in case Rebecca does not want to work things out.* He walked up behind her, walked around her to see her face, then he was shocked it was Rebecca he was looking at. He stood there momentarily looking at her and quickly walked away. He knew that she did not recognize him, he paid for his food and walked out in the parking lot and waited for Rebecca to come out on her way to a buggy to go home. They had a buggy taxi service.

He walked up to Rebecca and said, "Pardon me, I would like to give you these flowers." She started laughing and thanked him for it. Jonah looked at her and smiled and said, "Do You always take flowers from strangers?" Rebecca didn't know this was her husband, Jonah the prophet. Her mouth flew open; she couldn't believe she was stunned and in shock and said, "Is that you Jonah?"

"Yes it is me!"

"I can't believe what happened to you. What have you done to yourself?"

Jonah quickly responded and said "Yes, it was okay when you were taking flowers from a good-looking strange men right?" Rebecca looked at Jonah and said, "Well I don't know; yes you're good-looking; you're even better looking than I've ever seen you."

"This brand-new buggy is for you Rebecca. Two years, I've been hired by the cargo company. I will be leaving in the morning to go back to Nineveh to take cargo there, they will not recognize me. I bought these flowers for you. I can't believe how pretty you are. It can't be because I've been away that long? I came back to tell you that I was going to get a divorce from you. God told me it's okay if I do that."

Rebecca quickly responded in a harsh hateful voice, "No you cannot get a divorce from me. The Council and the congregation will never stand for it." Then Jonah said "Remember that the Council took me out and told me never to come back and if I did, they would call soldiers and put me in jail, remember, so that council has nothing to do with what I do."

"You told me the day after we got married you do not want to be a prophet's wife and you didn't believe I was a prophet of God, but you don't want to be a preacher's wife or prophet's wife and you still believe that, so why do you want to stay with someone you don't even like? It's like I've fallen in love with you Rebecca for the first time. It's like the first time I've even seen what you look like but that is not going to help because you don't believe anything I do, you don't like me, so I will get a divorce. Here are your flowers. Have a good day. We will go back to the house so I can see Luke and Kimberly."

Rebecca said, "Yes of course they miss you and they want to see you. They don't understand why you've done all of this to me, all of these bad things. You've hurt me so much and not taken care of me." Jonah looked at Rebecca and said, "There's a shipment of brand-new furniture being delivered to your house in the morning. I'm giving all that to you, the king gave me gold and I'm buying all of this new furniture and new clothes for you and the children.”

Rebecca said to Jonah, “The children have something they want to tell you when you get home.” On the way home, two ladies were riding in a buggy and passed by Rebecca and Jonah. One of the ladies spoke up very quickly Hi Rebecca and walked over closer to the buggy and looked at Jonah and said, “Your secret's safe with me. You’re Jonah the true prophet of God, I would know you anywhere. Remember me? I was blind and you prayed for me and God healed my eyes. We have some baked pies. Will bring them by tonight for supper. Jonah hugged the ladies and thanked them very much and looked forward to their pies.

Rebecca and Jonah were riding on toward the house when Rebecca said, “That lady is crazier than a fruitcake. She didn't get her eyes healed; she made all of that up.”   Jonah remained silent because he had told them many times they knew that it was true; the community knew that it was true and the medical records proved that this woman was blind; this was the bitterness and hatred that Rebecca had in her heart. Jonah's heart was ripped into the pain that he felt because he preached love to everyone but could not give love to his wife. He could not show it even though he tried.

Chapter 7

Jonah's Fish Ride

When Jonah got home, he opened the door and Luke and Kimberly came running. "Dad, Dad's home, Jonah the great prophet." They were excited and jumped in the arms of their dad and they hugged momentarily, laughing with tears running down the children's faces; they were so glad that their dad was home. Luke was jumping up and down. "Dad I have to tell you something. I have great news. I have to tell you something."

Jonah was laughing, "Yes son yes please tell me," Jonah said. "In Nineveh, they have an amusement park with all these fantastic rides and they have a new one called Jonas Fish Ride! Please take us, take us. We want to ride the fish ride please, Dad, take us to Nineveh so we can ride the fish ride. Please dad, you have your own amusement park right named after you, Jonas Fish Ride. I want to get inside the fish and ride like you did Dad," Luke said. Jonah bent down and took Luke and Kimberly in his arms and said, "Tomorrow, you're going with me on the cargo wagon. I'm taking you to Nineveh to ride that Jonah fish ride. What do you think about that?"

Luke and Kimberly were screaming, jumping up and down, happy with joy and said, "We're going to pack right now," and they ran off in the room and started packing. Rebecca looked at Jonah and said, "This is another one of your harebrained schemes to make up things, trying to act like a big shot. Running off just to get away from me to go do anything else."

Jonah looked to Rebecca and said, "You know you give me an idea. I think I'll go find that fish that I was in and see if I can move back in with it. that would be Better than being with you. I'm going to pack my bags and get ready to leave in the morning, you'll have all your new furniture early in the morning."

The next morning Jonah, Luke and Kimberly were on the cargo wagon speedily hurrying on their way to Nineveh. This was going to be a fast trip; they had to make the best time all day long. They stopped just enough time to make camp, cook a little supper and get up the next morning. After all, he was working for a cargo company and Jonah had to keep a schedule. They arrived in Nineveh once again.

"This trip went very fast," Luke said. "There it is, the amusement park and there's Jonah's fish ride. It is the biggest one in the whole amusement park." It was the biggest longline you'd ever seen. Luke got up there to get ready to get on it and he said, "Here's the real Jonah and that was swallowed by the real fish. That's my dad." Jonah said, "Luke don't tell anyone. Some people would be happy and some people would be mad, so go and have fun. I'll be right here because in the morning we have to go back to Jerusalem. I have other types of cargo to get back."

The next day, they quickly headed back to Jerusalem, where Jonah was getting set up with a live concert to sing and preach. A great crowd started coming around to hear Jonah. They didn't know this was Jonah; they just thought he was a good singer and preacher. That evening after the concert, Jonah was in his buggy on his way back to the hotel. He had already gotten a divorce from Rebecca and she quickly moved to another city.

When Jonah was on his way home to the hotel, a group of men grabbed hold of him, turned him over in his wagon and beat him with rods. Jonah was half dead; a stranger came the next morning and found him laying there half dead, picked him up and put him on his horse and took him to the hospital. Jonah lay very sick and broken up with a concussion and couldn't even walk; he was carried around.

The news flashed all over the synagogue in Jerusalem and into Nineveh, saying this was the great prophet? The Council gathered around and said, "This proves you're not a true prophet of God. All of these bad things would not happen to you if you were a true prophet of God. Look at us, we all have riches, we have much; we are the ones blessed by God. Jonah picked up his head and said, "Judgment day is coming."

When the shipmates nearby heard that Jonah the prophet lay in the hospital from injuries, they quickly went to see him. The news press printed all of the story and talked to the ship's captain and said, "It was Jonah's fault that you had a storm in the first place. Why would you come and see him in the hospital?" They said, "Because we know that Jonah is a true prophet of God and that he is right with God."

Chapter 8

Jonah's Hospital Visit

Many people in Jerusalem and leaders of the congregation knew in times past that Jonah the prophet had prophesied great things and they all came to pass. Jonah's best friend, Levi, was one of the former shipmates on the ship from Joppa that Jonah sailed on. The storm came up and the shipmates threw him overboard because Jonah told them to throw him out. He came in and said he believed that Jonah was a true prophet of God and saw many things and miracles. Jonah said to Levi, "I'm glad to see you. I'm glad you came."

Levi said, "I need to ask you something Jonah and I don't mean this in the wrong way. What I mean is I don't mean it like a lot of other people are saying these words. They're saying that if you were a true prophet of God, you would not be injured and laying in the hospital. They said after all if you were a true prophet of God, you would have miracles and not be sick. Nurses have to carry you to the examination room and back to your bad you can't even walk!"

Levi quickly stated, "I don't feel this way. You know I believe in you." Then he said, "Of course I want you to know I'm with you when you get to be rich and famous. I want to be with you, tell me Jonah, why have all these bad things happened to you if God spoke to you and told you, you will be rich and famous and be preaching and singing all over the world? God told you to go to Nineveh and preach in 40 days they would be overthrown, but Jonah that did not happen."

Then Jonah, being very weak, leaned up from the hospital bed, and said to Levi, "Will you follow the one who gives you the most money and gold, or the one that created the world and all the gold? When I prophesied to Jeroboam that he would prosper and have much riches, Jerusalem received the wealth, but they still did not serve God. When God sent me to Nineveh to preach in 40 days, Nineveh will be overthrown, and Nineveh repented and cried out to God. Jerusalem was jealous and mad Jerusalem was mad at me. Israel was angry with me because now they're getting wealthy and they have the blessing of God, and now they call me a false prophet, because Nineveh was spared!!"

Then Jonah said to Levi, "Will you go with me even if I have no money? Because I know God has called me and spoken to me, and I will do what God has told me to do. Thank you Levi, for coming to see me and talk to me. That means everything to me. When I am better and set up in preaching and singing, I hope you will be with me."

Chapter 9

Rebecca's Last Hospital Visit

Jonah's ex-wife, Rebecca came back to town to get the rest of her furniture as she moved to Nineveh. She went to the hospital with two ladies from the congregation to see Jonah. She came into Jonah's hospital room, and walked over to Jonah's bed, looked at him and said, "I came here to get the rest of my furniture. This is my last trip. I have moved to Nineveh. I wanted to see for one last time if we could work it out and get married again."

Then Rebecca spoke sharply to Jonah and said, "You need to admit that God is punishing you because you went to Joppa Bay and got on the ship and were going away from Nineveh instead of going to Nineveh." Jonah opened his eyes and said, "I see, I will ask you a question: how do you think God is punishing me for not going to Nineveh and preaching when you told me that God did not tell me to go to Nineveh!! You don't believe I am a prophet of God."

Rebecca responded, "Jonah I don't believe you are a prophet of God. I don't believe God told you to go to Nineveh." Jonah said, "Do you think God is punishing me for doing something that God did not tell me to do? Do you think God did not speak to me?"

"Jonah the congregational leaders said these horrible things would not happen to a prophet if he was really God's prophet."

Two of the ladies from the congregation came closer to Jonah's bed and said, "We will be praying for you Jonah because we don't want you to be sick." Jonah, holding his head up very weak, said, "Years ago when we came to your congregation, I preached and told you Rebecca, my ex-wife was not pregnant. I prophesied in two years, she would be pregnant and this child would be a girl!! After two years Rebecca was pregnant. I came back and preached, she was only a month away from having a baby girl. I asked her at that time to come up on the stage. I presented her to you and I declared two years before she was pregnant and now she's pregnant and this child is a girl, and I declare to you that after this child is born, I will bring her back to your congregation and prove that God told me we would have a little girl.   We left and four months later, I came back. When we came back I lifted up my little girl, Kimberly. Rebecca stood there before all of you when I was prophesying my little girl and Rebecca said stop saying that you're embarrassing me. And do you remember what I said when I stood before the Council? I told you that when I come back with my baby girl Kimberly that you would say it is a coincidence and not that God told me. The pastor begged me to repent and say the next night of the revival that I did not really mean what I said. The next night, I came to the revival and I stood before the congregation and I said to all of you that last night, everything that I prophesied will come to pass. I said that if it does not come to pass, you can call me a false prophet but when I bring my brand-new little girl back to you, you will say it's a coincidence. Anyway, when I prophesied King Jeroboam would prosper Jerusalem, you all rejoiced because you got more gold and food and cattle even though you didn't want to give me anything you are jealous and mad angry at me, because all those things came to pass. Now you're angry because all the Ninevites were not destroyed. You are the ones that wanted the Ninevites people to be killed and destroyed off the face of the earth, but not me. I love everyone, I love the Ninevites, I preached love to you, all the prophecies I preached, I preach love. God only chooses prophets that, he knows, love him and will follow him."

Jonah looked at Rebecca and said to her, "You must be Ken to Job's wife, because she's sad to Job curse God and die. That was not a nice thing to say she said that to Job because she had hate and anger in her heart. If she knew that Job was a perfect and upright man before God, she would have stood by his side and said you are going to get well and you're going to get more riches she was not with Job after that because she blamed Job because all of her children got killed and they lost everything. Job got double what he had before and he got a new wife."

The two ladies from the congregation turned around and, jerked their heads and said, "Let's get out of here. He's unreasonable and he's not right with God." Rebecca leaned over to Jonah very angrily and said, "I'm leaving now. I don't ever want to see you again and I just want you to know that God hates me anyway."

Rebecca started to walk away when Jonah said, "I would tell you one last thing you said to me the day after we got married. When we were on our way to a camp meeting where I was going to preach in prophesied, you said you did not want to be a preacher's wife. You did not want to marry a so-called prophet. You looked at me and said I was not a prophet anyway. I would have money to take care of my wife. I said, Rebecca, we dated for four years you went to revivals with me and now we wake up from our honeymoon with the congregation and you don't want to be a preacher's wife but you refused to get an annulment and told me that you would embarrass me to all the congregation that I could never preach again." Jonah said, "I wish the best for you, this conversation is over." Rebecca turned around and stormed out of the hospital, slamming things down the hallway and screaming at the top of her voice. That was the last time Jonah saw or heard from Rebecca.

The next morning, Jonah received a miracle: his body was healed. He jumped up out of bed, and got dressed and walked down the hall to the nurses' station. The doctors and nurses were having a meeting; they were going to inform Jonah's family that he was not going to live another day! A nurse turned around and said, "Sir can we help you? Do you need something?" Jonah said, "Yes I'm checking out of the hospital." The nurse turned around with a puzzled look on her face, "What do you mean checking out? You have never been in our hospital." Jonah said, "I am the patient from room 224. I am Jonah the prophet."

The doctor's mouth fell open; he said, "What? Let me look at you! It is Jonah the prophet!! How is this possible?" Jonah looked at them and said, "God gave me a miracle and now I am going to put up a tent at Joppa Bay and preach a tent revival. I would like for all of you to come. I'm going to have the best band there and I will be preaching."

The doctors said, "At least let us examine you one more time." But Jonah turned and said goodbye. Then he went to Levi's house and told him he had received a miracle in his body. He told Levi to get the band together and get the tent as they were going to Joppa Bay. Levi gathered the band together in the wagons and loaded up the tent and they went to Joppa Bay and set up the tent. Jonah had the press to print big signs saying, "Jonah will be preaching on the prayer Jonah prayed in the fish's belly."

The next night, Jonah's band was playing music. Over 2,000 people came to the tent revival. People were screaming and shouting and jumping for joy and rejoicing in God. People shouted loudly, "This is Jonah, the prophet of the living God. They made a fish ride of him in the amusement park in Nineveh, that great city that repented and turned to God." They yelled with loud voices, "Jonah can we have your autograph?"

Jonah quickly went to the people, signing autographs, hugging them, expressing their love for each other, and rejoicing in the Lord. Jonah started preaching, "Many lies have been told about me and my journey. The lies have been told about me, why I was swallowed by a fish, why I went to Joppa Bay, why I went to Nineveh and preached in 40 days Nineveh shall be overthrown. I will explain to you tonight why I went to Joppa Bay, why I was in the fish's belly, why the fish spit me out, and why I went to Nineveh and preach, and why I'm standing here today."

The congregation and was excited with anticipation; they had heard all the rumours and now at last, the prophet Jonah himself was explaining what happened. "I did not run from God when I went to Joppa Bay to get on a ship. I have the peace of God in my heart I have the peace of God in my heart. That's why I was able to go down to the bottom of a ship raging in the storm and sleeping peacefully. When I was inside the fish, I prayed this prayer and I will explain to you what I meant by the prayer. I prayed and said I cried by reason of my affliction unto the Lord. He heard me out of the belly of hell cried I and the Lord my heard my voice for thou hadst cast me into the deep in the midst of the sea of the floods compressed me about all thy billows. The waves passed over me and I said I am cast out of thy sight, yet I will look again toward the holy temple. At that moment, I thought I was going to die in the fish's belly. I did not say I repented, for going to Joppa Bay, my heart was always right with God. I praise the Lord with Thanksgiving in my mouth and I have vowed salvation is of the Lord. I did not say anywhere in my prayer that I needed a change of heart. My heart was always right with God. I was just giving Thanksgiving and saying with my mouth that I had already vowed salvation is of God, that God is my salvation from the belly of hell. I cried because I thought I was going to die. I did not even pray, I did not even pray and ask, God to get me out of the fish's belly!! I prayed even though I was out of the sight of God. I would pray and tell God that he is my salvation whether we live or die when we are God's were God's forever. Many people said when I was in the fish's belly that, I said God, I am sorry for going to Joppa Bay and getting on a ship I did not say that, because my heart was right with God. I thought I was going to die in the fish's belly and I went to the temple in my soul and in my spirit and I was having a revival in that fish's belly. I felt the presence of God around me and I knew that God was with me forever. I rejoiced and I praised God with my voice as loud as I could in that big old fish and then

God made the fish sick and he spit me out on dry land!! If I needed to repent, then I would have."

Chapter 10

Jonah Did Not Die!

Jonah continued preaching, "When I was in the fish's belly, I prayed a prayer to God; I did not die in the fish's belly, because a dead man cannot pray. If I did die in the fish's belly, then God raised me from the dead. That would be a miracle, that would be wonderful. God did not send a fish to swallow me to, teach me a lesson, or punish me, or prepare me to preach to the Ninevites. God did not call me to go and preach to Nineveh to make me a better man or to make me closer to God. God called me to go to Nineveh and called me to be God's prophet because God loves me and God knew that I love him, before

I went to Nineveh!! That's why I preached the love of God to all people before I preached to Jeroboam the second and to all Israel before I went to Nineveh. I knew Israel did not want me to go and preach to Nineveh. I did not run from Nineveh because I did not want the Ninevites to perish. I knew that God would spare the Ninevites even if I did not go. When I was in the belly of the fish, I thought that I was going to die and go on to heaven. That is the vow that I made salvation is of the Lord and I knew I was saved even though I was going to die in the fish's belly. God's love is everlasting. I knew God loved me before I started on the journey to Nineveh. When I came to Joppa Bay to get on a ship, I was not running from God. God called me to be a prophet and chose me to go to Nineveh for the benefit of all the unbelievers in Jerusalem and the unbelievers and Nineveh. I knew if I had died in the fish's belly God would raise up Ninevites to be spared. After I preached in Nineveh, I went up on the East Hill and I watched the Ninevites when they repented and was rejoicing and was glad that they were not overthrown. I was only angry at Jerusalem, and the Ninevites that was going to take advantage of God's blessing and not serve God in their hearts and not worship the one true God that created the heavens and the earth, the lying vanities of those who worship gold buildings there abundance of prosperity but they don't worship the creator, the God of heaven and earth. Then God gave me a miracle and grew me a plant and showed me by an example that heaven was in me and the miracles he wanted to give me and prosper me and that is true, prophets were going to receive blessings and that I would not just be looked at as a prophet anymore. But God was going to show the world's blessing upon me, the poor little prophet swallowed by a fish. I want you to know all of Israel, this was for your benefit because I knew in my heart, that God is love!"

Chapter 11

God's Riches

Jonah continued preaching, "You can give everyone diamonds and gold and silver and rubies and all riches but that will not make you love God!!

Loving for God only comes from your heart if you want to love God; then suddenly, soldiers came rushing into the tent and grabbed Jonah. They started dragging him from the back. Some of the people that were in the revival shouted yes, take Jonah, and kill him. Most of the people in the tent revival believed Jonah and knew that he was a true prophet of God. Jonah shouted when they were taking him away, "No matter what you do to me, you cannot stop me from loving you."

Jonah was put in the local jail they brought him before the Council. The next day some people shouted, "Execute Jonah! Kill him!" When the king of Nineveh heard that Jonah was in jail and they were going to execute him, he quickly assembled a team of horses and soldiers and rode to Jerusalem as fast as he could. The king of Nineveh spoke to the king of Jerusalem, and said to Jerusalem, "We will set up a trade agreement that will prosper both of our cities. We ask that you let Jonah go and live and preach. He preached to our people and Nineveh was spared. We have herbs and spices, building materials, tents and, fresh garden vegetables, and a lot of cattle for a fair price. Jeroboam the second agreed and said, "There will be peace between our cities. No one will set A had against Jonah again he is free to preach and say in all the nations we will support and backup and declare that Jonah is a true prophet of God."

Chapter 12

Jonah's Riches

Jonah quickly was preaching to hundreds of thousands of people. Jonah had an abundance of riches, golden jewellery, rubies, tents and fine houses, and chariots, and all the people that said bad things about Jonah and called him names and called a false prophet, and said that those things were not true came and begged Jonah to be in his band, to be on his staff to work for him. They told Jonah, "Remember we are your friends!" Many of those were the ones who called in the congregational leaders to have Jonah arrested and put in jail, but now that Jonah was rich and famous, they told everyone they were always

Jonah's good friends. They always knew that Jonah would be rich and famous they would stay by his side forever. They came to his great big tent revivals; they came up to the front telling people they would do anything that Jonah wanted them to do, but when Jonah was being dragged away to be put in prison, they said, kill him they said, kill him he's a false prophet, but now they act like they love Jonah. They talked behind his back; they said bad things about Jonah all the time to all the other people. They told the newspaper and the press that they did good things by saying these bad things. Apparently, they did not know the difference between saying something good things or something bad about someone."

And when the soldiers came to drag Jonah away to put them in jail, they said, "We are doing this for your own good. We are doing this to help you because we love you Jonah. We know that you love everyone, so we will work for you now!" And that day, the soldiers would have killed Jonah. Then how could these people work for Jonah the prophet if he had died that day?

Jonah lifted up his eyes at the audience and said with a loud voice, "Now these people sound like Job's wife and my former wife Rebecca and my trouble. In my weakness, in my sickness, when I could not even get out of bed, Rebecca said it would be better off if I was dead and going to heaven. Of course she meant that in a very nice and very good way. So my answer and declaration before Israel is no, you cannot work for me because you really hate me! And you hate God, if you love God, you will love his prophets and you will believe his prophets."

Jonah quickly called his security and said, "Help these people out of my tent and out of my sight because they are not right with God." Jonah's security took these evil people and said, "Can you find the door by yourself or do you need some help? They turned and were shouting back at Jonah, "You're making the biggest mistake you ever made, where the best friend you ever had these people here. They don't really love you, and they're just here because you're giving them lots of money. We are going to take you to the court? Jonah we are going to sue you." Jonah said, "How would you sue me for money if you got me killed? Thank you very much. Have a good day."

Jonah continued preaching the presence of God was in this tent because everyone else was in one mind and one accord. People were shouting victory under God. They had the love of God in the tent. Everyone loved each other was shouting and laughing and joy because they knew the kingdom of God had come into that tent. Jonah shouted all the prophets of God had received the first fruits from heaven, and the people shouted with victory. The people of Jerusalem did not know they could feel the love of God and the love of each other more than they ever had. They did not know they could feel the love of God for now and forever, because Jonah had been preaching the kingdom of God. He preached heaven to Jerusalem; the prosperity that God wants to give his people is heaven in the kingdom of God; many things will happen on earth there will be a final kingdom of God, all things will be fulfilled all things will come to pass, that was prophesied the kingdom of God has always been in plain sight for everyone to see the kingdom of God is in the light; only people in the darkness cannot see the kingdom of God; now they will have joy and peace and harmony, the true children of God will have the kingdom of heaven in their hearts they will live every day like the kingdom of God rules their life. Then Jonah looked in the back of the tent. The soldiers that came and dragged him away and took him to jail before came running down to the front and they begged Jonah, "Please forgive us for what we did. We are sorry, we want to be your friend and stand by you."

Jonah hugged the soldiers; they were crying and laughing, they were telling each other they loved each other. People were shouting the victory and they said, "So this is what heaven is like!" And Jonah said, "Yes this is heaven. We will live every day just like this. The enemies of God that try to destroy the house of God will be overthrown. There will be other prophets after me they will literally preach destruction to evil cities that come against God's prophets, but rejoice now Israel and all the people, because you can see the kingdom of God."

There was joy all through the land as the people rejoiced. Jonah had a lot of friends in love, and the true friends that were with Jonah. They all loved God in their hearts and were very happy. Then all the sudden" there was a loud noise at the back of the tent when they seen soldier, come in with the King of Nineveh the King walk up to the front stage where Jonah was standing, He just looked at Jonah, and then he said, there was one more thing I wanted to give you" then from behind the King came walking out with a vail over there face Then Jonah said my King who is this. Then the King removed there vail off their face, Jonah could not believe it was Honey standing there the King said I give Honey to you to be your wife, I took her from the council, they ran to each other arms everyone was happy.

The End